When You Remember Deir Yassin

عندما تتذكرون دير ياسين

Poems
R. L. Green

Translated into Arabic by
Kristin Peterson-Ishaq and Mousa Ishaq

Fomite
Burlington, VT

Poems copyright 2014 © by R. L. Green
Translations copyright 2014 © by Kristin Peterson-Ishaq and Mousa Ishaq

With permission:
"If We Can" translated by Amar Tawakkalna
"Hear, O Israel: Gaza Is Human!" translated by A. Reem Aldakheel

All rights reserved. No part of this book may be reproduced in any form or by any means without the prior written consent of the publisher, except in the case of brief quotations used in reviews and certain other noncommercial uses permitted by copyright law.

ISBN-13: 978-1-937677-05-3
Library of Congress Control Number: 2013943027

Fomite
58 Peru Street
Burlington, VT 05401
www.fomitepress.com

Cover and interior art - Peter Schumann

When You Remember Deir Yassin

عندما تتذكرون دير ياسين

To Suze Rotolo and Miriam Ward, RSM
Friends to the Oppressed
and Lovers of Truth

جدول المحتويات

2	عندما تتذكرون دير ياسين
8	1956
14	بسببكم أنتم وفلسطين
20	المسألة اليهودية كلها
24	الأباتشي في غزة
28	عندما تطحنون الكعب
32	ليس إلا الليمون والليم
34	إلى إمان الهمص
36	الجدار يشرح فلسطين
42	لو كنا نستطيع
46	أتحدث عن فلسطين
50	موت غزة موتاً سريعاً
56	عابود الود يعة
60	صفِّقوا بأيديكم لفلسطين
66	هل تريد أن تناقش إذا هذه إبادة جماعية أم لا؟
72	يا ! فلسطين!
76	إلى أشرف أبي رحمة
82	يوم الإثنين في فلسطين
88	فلتسمعي يا إسرائيل إن أهل غزة لبشر!
92	إنهم يجعلونا نشعر كأننا لا شيء
96	لا تسرقوا

Table of Contents

When You Remember Deir Yassin	3
1956	9
Because of You People and Palestine	15
The Whole Jewish Thing	21
Apaches in Gaza	25
When You Grind the Heel	29
Just Lemons and Limes	33
For Iman Al-Hams	35
Wall Slices Palestine	37
If We Can	43
I Speak of Palestine	47
Gaza Dying Quickly	51
Gentle Aboud	57
Clap Hands For Palestine	61
You Want to Quibble Over Whether or Not It's Genocide?	67
O! Palestine!	73
For Ashraf Abu Rahmeh	77
Palestine Monday	83
Hear, O Israel: Gaza is Human!	89
They Make Us Feel Like We Are Nothing	93
Steal Not	97
Translator's Note	100

عندما تتذكرون دير ياسين

مرحباً يا ريفكي! هالو! مرحباً يورام، مالكا، أفيشاي،
مرحباً كاتسيا، مارئيون، ياهوشواً، يائيل.
كيف حالك؟ هَوْ آرْ يو؟
أصدقاء أحباء لأبي وأمي منذ خمسين عام——
متى أزوركم في تل أبيب؟ في زخرون يأكوف؟
متى أسير معكم في كروم العنب؟ ومتى أقابل أحفادكم؟
ومتى أتعرف على الصهر الذي يبيع البلوجينز؟
عندما تتذكرون دير ياسين

ولماذا أوجه كلامي إليكم باللغة العربية المحطمة؟
أكيداً أقدرأن أقول «شلوم، ما شلوم خا؟» باللغة العبرانية؟
وهكذا أظهر أحترامي لكم كما أودّ أن أشعره
وقد نتعانق في المطار
ونتعشى من جديد تحت عرائش محملة بخمر السنة المقبلة،
ومن جديد نمر صامطون بين الذكريات
المحفوظة في ياد فاشيم
عندما تتذكرون دير ياسين

ويمكن أن نأكل البرتقال من الشجر الذي زرعته أمي
تحت نظركم في عام 1953
عندما تتذكرون دير ياسين.

When You Remember Deir Yassin

Marhaba Ya Rifka! Hello! Marhaba Yoram, Malka, Avishai,

Marhaba K'tsia, Marion, Yehoshua, Yaël.

Keef hal-ak? How are you?

Beloved friends of my father and mother for 50 years –

When will I visit you in Tel Aviv? In Zichron Ya'aqov?

When will I walk in your vineyards? Meet your grandchildren?

Meet the son-in-law in the blue jeans business?

When you remember Deir Yassin

And why do I address you in halting Arabic?

Surely I can say "Shalom, Ma sh'lom cha?" in Hebrew?

This would show the respect I long to feel

We could embrace at the airport

Dine again under arbors laden with next year's wine

We would again pass silently among memories

Enshrined at Yad Vashem

When you remember Deir Yassin

We can eat oranges from trees my mother planted

As you watched in 1953.

When you remember Deir Yassin.

وميكن أن نتحدث عن أصدقائكم وعائلاتكم
نتحدث عن آبسالوم الإبن الغالي لدافيد شوهام
الذي قتل في حرب على الدولات المجاورة،
ونتحدث عن روثي الزوجة الأولى لياهوشوأ
التي توفت في حادث هجوم على مطار في الستينات.
ونتحدث عن صديقكم دافيد تيدهار
الذي أقعدني في حضنه وأنا عمري ست سنوات
وفاخر بقطع حناجر فلسطينية
في القدس، حين كان رئيس البوليس
في 1948.
كل هذا ميكن أن نفعله

عندما تتذكرون دير ياسين

We can talk about your friends and family

About David Shoham's precious Absalom

Slain in a war against neighboring states

About Yehoshua's first wife Ruthie,

Dead in an airport attack in the '60's.

We can talk about your friend David Tidhar

Who sat me on his lap when I was six

And bragged of slitting Palestinian throats

In Jerusalem, when he was chief of police

In 1948.

All this we can do

When you remember Deir Yassin.

1956

تمزح أمي أمام الكاميرة

في زي فتاة الحريم العربي على أسلوب ديزني

تحت شجر الزيتون

في زخرون يأكوف المشمّسة

والعام ألف وتسع مئة وستة وخمسين.

صاحبة البيت ريفكي الكريمة

تحبّ الخادمة جدا

(وهي عندها منذ الطفولة، ودائما عند ركبتها،)

ولكن يقال إنها

تصفعها صفعات جامدة.

وأعرف أنهم زرعوا برتقالاً

لقد ذقته بنفسي

في عام ألف وتسع مئة وستة وثمانين

أسابيع في وسط تشرين الثاني

ورتّبت رحلة إلى "إسرائيل،"

دفعا أبي وأمي عنها، وأنا

المغفّل قبلت مع أنّي كنت أجهّز أن أكون أربعين من عمري

أب عنده شهادة.

وعلى طرق لوس أنجيليس العامة

من تل أبيب

8

1956

Mother frolics for the camera

In a Disney Arab harem girl's costume

Under olive trees

In Sunny Zichron Ya'aqov.

And it's nineteen fifty-six.

Gracious hostess Rifka

Loves her servant dearly

(she's been with her since childhood, always at the knee,)

And yet is said

to slap her quite severely.

I know they planted oranges

I've tasted them myself

in nineteen eighty-six

Middle weeks November

A tour arranged to "Israel,"

Paid for by my parents, and I the

fool accepted, though preparing to be forty

A father with degree.

On the L.A. highways

From Tel Aviv

إلى فلسطين

إلى يافا،

إلى البحر عند أشكيلون

شاحنات عمال غاضبين يتعلّمون ان يحدّقوا كأنهم في شرق لوس أنجيليس

غزّة مثل جوهانيسبورج

غزّة مثل البرونكس

والبرتقال على أرض من؟

أين توجد جودييا بالضبط؟

متى نحن في الضفة الغربية؟

لماذا لا الخليل

لماذا لا غزة

ودليلنا جندي عجوز

سجنه الأنجليز

حارب في ثمانية وأربعين

ويعانق البدو وهو يكلمهم بالعربية

نتجول في ميرسيديس

نحن الأربع فقط

مصاحبنا هذا السائق

مسلح وما زال خطرا،

يتصل بوحدته، مع أنه فوق الخمسة وسبعين.

تشريب سياسي على كل موقف، تركيب

أسطورة:

To Palestine

To Jaffa,

To the sea at Askelon

Trucks of angry workers learn to stare like East L.A.

Gaza like Johannesburg

Gaza like the Bronx

Oranges on whose land?

Where exactly is Judea?

When are we in the West Bank?

Why not Hebron

Why not Gaza

Our guide an ancient soldier

Imprisoned by the British

He fought in forty-eight

Hugs Bedouins in Arabic

We travel by Mercedes

Just the four of us

Accompanied by this driver

Armed and still a danger,

he checks in with his unit, though he is more than seventy-five.

Indoctrination every stop, a building

Of a tale:

"روبرت، هل تقدر أن تقرأ العبراني؟ ثم كيف؟

من أبيك الحبيب

الذي يعطي كثيرا إلى صهيون

وأخيراً أحضرك

وشقيقتك

لتشهدا محلات البلد والضواحي

التي لورد روتتشيلد ساعدنا في قهرها

يا لها من حلاوة أموال المؤسسات

'يا له من حسن خيمك ورعيتك

يا يعقوب.' "

"Robert, can you read the Hebrew? Then how?

From your beloved father

Who gives so much to Zion

At last he's brought you

And your sister

To see the mall and suburbs

Lord Rothschild helped us conquer

O! sweet foundation monies

'How Goodly are thy tents, and thy flocks

O! Jacob.' "

بسببكم أنتم وفلسطين

بسببكم أنتم وفلسطين لا أعود أن أعشّب حديقتي
وحتى أني أزيل العشب من حول الطماطم بحذر
"إلى موقع مفيد اكثر"
فيه "يمكن أن ينمو بين أشكالها"
يذكّرني بفلسطين جداً
يذكّرني بالجرائم ضد الإنسانية (ومن سيُشمل بها؟)
تمتدّ اليوم في مخيّم عائدة
واليوم قبل ذلك، في قبية، دير ياسين
صبرا وشاتيلا وجنين وطولكرم
هل يجب أن أواصل الكلام؟
نعم. غزة.
من فضلكم إسمعوا
جثث
مدنيون غير مسلحين
أطفال أطفال أطفال أطفال
لن أسحق نملة في مطبخي،
فقط لأني أقدر
لآني بالحاجة إلى "ليبينسروم"
لأني أزلت غابتها
وركبت فيها منضدتي بالفسيفساء،
والنملة هذه في طريقة غير ملائمة--وحتى
لا تحاول أن تسكن هناك--

Because of You People and Palestine

Because of you people and Palestine I can no longer weed my garden.

Even carefully moving the crabgrass from around my tomato plants

"To a more advantageous location"

in which "they can thrive amongst their own kind"

reminds me too much of Palestine

of crime against humanity (who shall be included?)

expanding today in Aida

the day before, in Qibya, Deir Yassin

Sabra and Shatilla and Jenin and Tulkarim

Must I go on?

Yes. Gaza.

Please listen

Dead bodies

Unarmed civilians

Children children children children

I won't crush an ant in my kitchen,

Just because I can

Because I need Lebensraum

Because I removed his forest

And put in my tiled counter,

On which he inconveniently – doesn't even

Try to live there –

بل تريد أن تمشي لثانية

لتصل إلى الكسرة

التي تركتها هناك؛

هل أقتلها لذلك؟

هل أسمّم طعامها؟

يذكّرني جداً بفلسطين

العراق وجوانتانامو

يذكّرني جداً بأفغانستان

بما صار في منظمة "موف" في فيلادلفيا

قنبلة من السماء

أسجنوا المنكوبين

لوموا الضحايا

إسرقوا مقابرهم

حتى لن أتدخل في رحلة النملة الصغيرة

لن أؤخّرها عند حاجز تفتيش

أو أغيّر طريقها في العالم

لن أفترض أن عندي حقوقاً أكثر منها

فقط لأني جديد هنا

غريب، مخرّب

فاتح.

يذكّرني جداً بفلسطين

بالنساء، العجائز والمرضى

بالأطفال--

نعم، الأطفال الفلسطينيون

just wants to walk for a second

across to the crumb

I left there;

should I kill him for that?

Shall I poison his food?

Reminds me too much of Palestine

Iraq and Guantanamo

Reminds me too much of Afghanistan

Of Move in Philadelphia

Bomb from the air

Jail the survivors

Blame the dead

Steal their graves

I won't even interfere with the ant's little journey,

won't delay him at a checkpoint

or alter his path through the world

Won't assume I have more rights than he does

Just because I'm new here

An alien, a destroyer

A conqueror.

Reminds me too much of Palestine

Of women, the old and the sick

of the children –

Yes, Palestinian Children

مثل أطفالكم

أحسن من أطفالكم

من ناحية التأدب والمساعدة،

الشهامة والشجاعة،

الحب والكرامة.

Like your own

Better than yours,

As far as manners and helping,

heart and courage,

Love and honor.

المسألة اليهودية كلها

"المسألة اليهودية كلها،"

قال صديق لي من قبيلة التشيروكي،

"هي أنّا 'لن نذهب إلى حجر الغاز مرة أخرى بدون قتال.'

"ولكنهم يريدون أن يرتكبوا هذا الشئ على الفلسطينيين

ثم يتضايقون إذا سمعوا الأنين

ولا تذكر الحجارة التافهة

التي تقذف لقيس وجود الكبرياء

عن هذا الظلم الذي يسحق هذا الشعب.

وينصحون، 'إرقصوا رقص سلام جميل،'

مثل المتسامحون الذين كانوا سابقاً ويودّون لو يكونوا ثانياً

'وضجّوا ضجّة فولكلورية مثل قبيلة الهوبي:

(وهذه أغنية تقدرون أن تغنوها)

"سامحوني إذا كنت واقفاً في طريق

جرافتكم الكاتيبيلر

سامحونا إذا كنا واقفين في طريق مستعمرتكم

شارعكم لليهود فقط

لأني واقف في طريق بركتكم للسباحة

التي توجد على نظرة من حصيدي المنهوب الذي قتله القحط؛

وفي طريق الأطفال اليهود المتمتعين بالصحة وهم يلعبون،

ونعم، سامحوني إذا أريتكم إبني

المجلود بمسدّس

والمغتصب الذي عنده أربعة عشر عاماً

The Whole Jewish Thing

"The whole Jewish thing,"
Said my Cherokee friend,
"Is 'we won't go to the gas chambers again without a fight,'
but they want to do this thing to the Palestinians.
And they get offended if they hear the moaning
Not to mention paltry stones
Thrown to measure pride's existence
About this oppression that's crushing this people.
'Do a pretty peace dance,' they advise,
like the liberals they once were, and would dearly like to be again
'and make folkloric noises like the Hopi:
(here's a song that you can sing)

    "pardon me for getting in the way

    of your Caterpillar bulldozer

    pardon us for getting in the way of your settlement

    your Jewish-only road

    for getting in the way of your swimming pool

    in sight of my drought-killed vandalized crop;

    in the way of healthy Jewish children playing,

    and yes, pardon me for showing you

    my pistol-whipped

    and raped fourteen year old son

وعلى زوجتي الميتة، التي طعنت في قلبها

بقطعة غليظة من بابنا الأمامي

الباب الذي فجَّرتموه بدلا من تقرعون عليه

لو علمتم كيف كنا أطعمناكم

لو قرعتم...".' '"

my dead wife, pierced through her heart

by a chunk of our front door

which you exploded instead of knocking

if only you knew how we would have fed you

had you knocked…" ' "

الأباتشي في غزة

تطلق هليكوبترات الاباتشي النار على ملاعب

حافلة بأطفال،

حافلة بمعلمين

بينما قبيلة الأباتشي الحقيقيين

يعانون من صحة سيئة

ومن مدارس منكسرة،

الثروة الأمريكية

مستهلكة في قتل غزة،

يحيا الشعب

الشعب الأمريكي،

متدرّبون على الحماقة.

Apaches in Gaza

Apache copters fire on playgrounds

filled with children,

filled with teachers

while the real Apaches

have bad health

broken schools,

American wealth

used up killing Gaza,

Viva La Raza

American People,

trained to be fools.

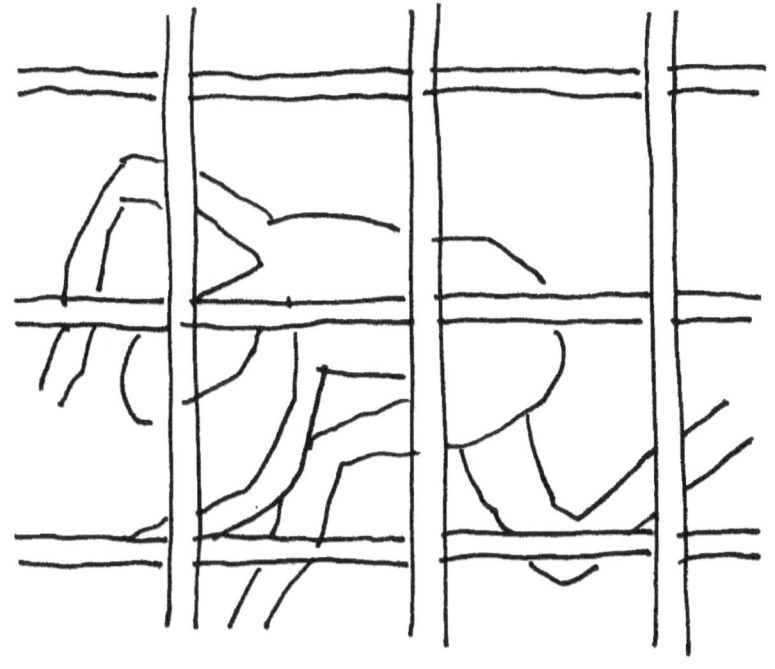

عندما تطحنون الكعب

عندما تطحنون الكعب
لدولتكم اليهودية المدعية هذه
علي براجم الأطفال الطرية
وأعرف أنكم فعلتم ذلك
ورأيتكم
كلنا رأيناكم

". . . إكسروا عظام
رامين الحجارة"
حجارة ضد بنادق
جنود رابين الأربعة
على ولد عنده عشر سنوات
يعدو
طقّوا يده على "سي.أن.أن."
مرة بعد مرة
كأنها غصنة
آلام جريمة
يا رابين ثم قُتلت أنت
لأنك كنت طيباً جداً،

وبعض الأحيان
الناس الذين تطحنوهم

When You Grind the Heel

When you grind the heel

Of your supposedly Jewish State

Into soft children's knuckles

And I know you did

And I saw you

We all did

"…break the bones

of the stone throwers"

stones against guns

Rabin's four soldiers

on a ten-year-old

he runs

snapped his arm on CNN

over and over

like kindling

agony crime

Rabin you then killed

For being too kind,

sometimes

the people you grind

يتخلون عن الحياة

يحرقون أنفسهم حرقاً

يخرجون سكينة

في السوق

وأنتم الهدف

وتفرّون

مقاهي

أوتوبوسات

كيف قدروا أن يفعلوا ذلك؟

كيف نقدر نحن؟

Abandon life

Burn themselves up

Pull a knife

In the market

You the target

you flee

cafes

buses

How could they?

How can we?

ليس إلا الليمون والليم

توفت أنتي سلمى

أم فلسطينية

بعيدة عن مسقط رأسها

غير متذمّرة

وبناتها وإبنها فركوا ورق الليم والليمون الطازه

من قوار مزروعة في البيت

وشمموها رائحته في النهاية

نكهة بلدها

ليست الحرب

ليس الإنفصال

ليس إلا الليمون والليم

وكانت وجبتها الأخيرة هي الفول الأخضر

ملقوط حديثاً من بستان إبنها

في فيرمونت

لا في عابود

لا في القدس

لا في الغربة

ليس إلا الليمون والليم

ليس إلا الحرية

Just Lemons and Limes

Auntie Salma has died

A Palestinian mother

Far from home

Not complaining

Her daughters and son crushed fresh lime and lemon leaves

From potted plants

And held them to her nose at the last

An aroma of home

Not war

Not separation

Just lemons and limes

Her last meal was foule

Picked fresh in her son's garden

In Vermont

Not in Aboud

Not in al-Quds

Not exile

Just lemons and limes

Just freedom

إلى إمان الهمص

"إسرائيلي مبرّأ من وفاة فتاة عربية"
خمس عشرة رصاصة في روح فلسطين
خمس عشرة رصاصة في جسم طفلة جميلة
سائرة إلى المدرسة
وكتبها في شنطة
في منطقة أعلن أن التجول فيها ممنوع
للفلسطينيين.

"لم نتوقع كثيراً من هذه المحكمة،"
يقول عمها.
خمس عشرة رصاصة في قلب اللياقة
عندما وقعت إلى الأرض،
تقول جريدة النيويورك تايمز،
النقيب "ر،"
(وحذفت السلطات إسمه
لحماية حقه للخصوصية)
تقرب منها وأطلق عليها
خمس عشرة رصاصة في طفلة مقتولة
خمس عشرة رصاصة في قلب السلام.

For Iman Al-Hams

"Israeli cleared in death of Arab girl"
Fifteen bullets into the soul of Palestine
Fifteen bullets into the body of a lovely child
Walking to school
With her books in a bag
In an area declared off limits
To Palestinians.

"We were not expecting much from this court,"
says her uncle.
Fifteen bullets into the heart of decency
As she fell to the ground,
Says the New York Times,
Captain "R,"
(name deleted by the authorities
To protect his privacy)
Approached her and fired
Fifteen bullets into a murdered child
Fifteen bullets into the heart of peace.

الجدار يشرح فلسطين

الجدار يشرح فلسطين،

جدار، سياج، حرام إنساني

الجدار يسرق ماء

الجدار يفصل بلداً

الجدار يبني كذباً

يدعي أنه يوقّف قنابل

الجدار يسرق حقولاً

من مزارعين سلميين

يوقّف والدين

من وصولهما إلى المستشفى

ومعهما طفل يموت

ويحوّط بلداً

يترك ضحايا على الطرفين.

لأمن مَن

يطالب هذا السجن؟

الجدار سارق

الجدار قاتل

الجدار يعطي للمستعمرين

آباراً مسروقة

كروما مسروقة.

Wall Slices Palestine

Wall slices Palestine,

Wall, fence, human shame

wall steals water

wall divides town

wall builds lies

claims to stop bombs

wall steals fields

from peaceful farmers

stops parents

from reaching hospital

with dying child

encircles town

leaves victims on both sides.

whose security

demands this prison?

wall thief

wall killer

wall gives settlers

stolen wells

Stolen orchards.

يقتل الحضارة

يتهم إتهاماً عنصرياً

يرتكب الإبادة الجماعية

إقرؤا التعريف

يتشدق دعاية

لا يقدر الجدار أن يقتل الحقيقة

جدار جريمة

حرام جدار

إهدموا الجدار

إستعملوا الحجارة

في البستان

غذّوهما الإثنين

kills civilization

makes racist accusation

commits genocide

Read the definition

Mouths propaganda

wall can't kill truth

wall crime

shame wall

Tear wall down

Use stones

In garden

nourish both

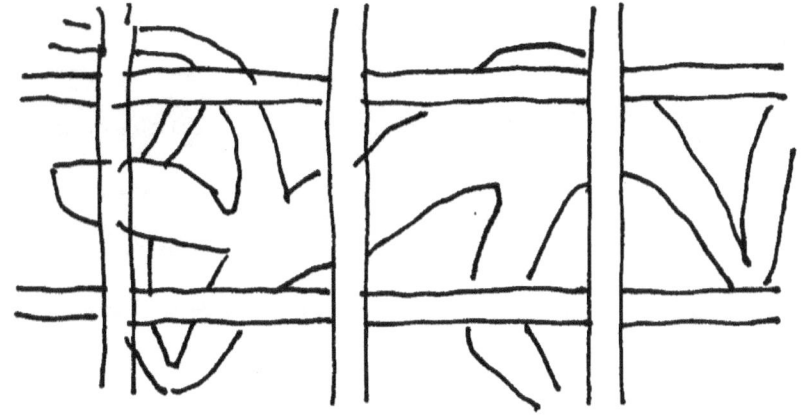

لو كنا نستطيع

مقيدٌ ومعصوبُ العينين
ومأخوذٌ إلى مكانٍ مجهول
مقيدٌ ومعصوبُ العينين
رأسُه مغطىً ومهملٌ ومخفي
خصوصيةُ التعذيبِ
تدميرُ الصفاتِ المحببةِ
الرجالُ المسنونَ والبناتُ الصغيراتُ
أخواتُهم وأبناؤهم
مدعوونَ إلى رصاصةٍ
جالوت يقتلُ داود
مع أنَّ الحجارةَ لم تُرمَ على الجسدِ
الدولةُ الأثيرةُ والأسلحةُ المسيطرةُ
التي خلفَها الجنودُ الغاضبونَ
تنفقُ وقتَها لتَقهَر الأطفالَ
كاسرةٌ قلوبَ الأمهاتِ
في بيتَ لحمَ ونابُلسَ
مقيدٌ ومعصوبُ العينين
ومأخوذٌ إلى مكانٍ مجهول
مؤسسةٌ لا اسمَ لها
لا تُقيِّدُ وحشيتَها
آدابُ السلوكِ ولا الدناءة
مقيدٌ ومعصوبُ العينين

If We Can

handcuffed and blindfolded

and taken to an unknown location

handcuffed and blindfolded

hooded lost and hidden

privacy of torment

wasting lovely kind

old men small girls

their brothers and their sons

tempted to a bullet

Goliath killing David

for stones thrown not at flesh

intending State and finding steel

behind which angry soldiers

take time to conquer children

breaking mother's souls

in Bethlehem and Nablus

handcuffed and blindfolded

and taken to an unknown location

an enterprise unnamed

ferocity unbound

by decency or sloth

handcuffed and blindfolded

أنتَ لسْتَ مجهولاً

نحنُ نفكرُ بك

ونرى عينيك

ونريدُك أَنْ تعود

مازِلنا نُحبُّك

ولنْ ننساك

نريد أن نَجِدك

وأَنْ نحرِرَك

وأَنْ نحتَفِظَ بك

لو كنا نستطيع

ترجمة: عمار توكلنا

you are not unknown

we think of you

we see your eyes

we want you back

we love you still

we won't forget

we want to find you

and to free you

and to hold you

if we can

Translated into Arabic by Amar Tawakkalna

أتحدث عن فلسطين

أتحدث عن إصراركم على

التصديق بما يقال لكم

إن تكونوا عمياً إلى هذه الدرجة:

أكيد تعلمتم

كيف لا تعرفون

إن تكونوا بلا إحساس إلى هذه الدرجة حتى تقدروا أن تقولوا إن

"هؤلاء الناس يستحقون أن يكونوا

داخل هذه المقبرة."

لا يقدرون أن يتحركوا

أو يحيوا

أو يطعموا

ونعم،

أتحدث عن فلسطين.

لا تقدرون أن تعتقدوا أن

مصيرها عادل

بدون أن تشتركوا

في طحن

عظامهم ودمائهم

لخلطها بأرض الصحراء

وبزيت الزيتون

لكي تبنوا دولتكم، سجنكم؛

I Speak of Palestine

I speak of your insistence

on believing what you're told

to be so blind:

you must have learned

what not to know

to be so cold that you can say

"These people do belong

inside this tomb."

They cannot move

or live

or eat

And, yes,

I speak of Palestine.

You cannot hold

its fate is just

and not be part

of grinding up

their bones and blood

to mix with desert earth

and olive oil

to build your state, your jail;

يحيط جدار

بمكانهم، هكذا:

غرفة تعذيب

حقل جائع

دار مسروق

درع بشري

رصاصة لطفل

وغاز سام في شوارع قروية

طعامهم، طعامهم!

زال طعامهم

تطهّرون

وتدفعون

وتعاقبون

آخذون ما تريدون

لتملكوه لوحدكم.

إننا نعرف أنه جريمة الإغتصاب،

ومع إن العالم يسجّل

أسماءكم وأعمالكم،

المجالس والمحاكم القادمة

لن تحي

الموتى والمشردين والمفقودين.

ونعم، أتحدث عن فلسطين

a wall surrounds

their place, like this:

a torture room

a starving field

a stolen home

a human shield

a bullet for a child

and poison gas on village streets

their food, their food!

Their food is gone

you cleanse

and push

and punish

taking what you want

to have for you alone.

We know it's rape,

and though the world records

your names and deeds,

the future courts and trials

will not revive

the dead, displaced and missing.

And yes, I speak of Palestine

تموت غزة موتاً سريعاً

تموت غزة موتاً سريعاً
عطشانة وجائعة
بحر قريب
لسان يكسوه الملح
فم مفتوح
عيون متغيّمة

إرسلوا شيئاً إلى غزة
وإلّا نتركها تقع
إلى الرصاص يومياً
تقتل الأطفال
وعالم صابر
يطالب ببرهان أكثر

من أجساد عريانة
قتلت بالرصاص عند الإطلاع
ومساجين معذبين
معرّين وجلدهم مسلوخ
تهاجمهم الكلاب

لحرب الربح
ولطوفان النفط الغامق

Gaza Dying Quickly

Gaza dying quickly

parched and starving

sea close by

tongue caked with salt

mouth open

cloudy eyes

Send something to Gaza

else we let it fall

to bullets daily

killing children

a patient world

demands more proof

Than naked bodies

shot on sight

prisoners tortured

stripped and flayed

set on by hounds

Of profit's war

of oil's dark flood

ولدَيْن إسرائيل
الآن مدفوع بالدماء

وعالم في الصمت
لا كل دولة
ولكن أكثريتها
راضية أن ترى
ثانياً
إبادة جماعية.

and Israel's debt

now paid by blood

a world in silence

not every nation

yet more than most

content to see

another

mass extermination.

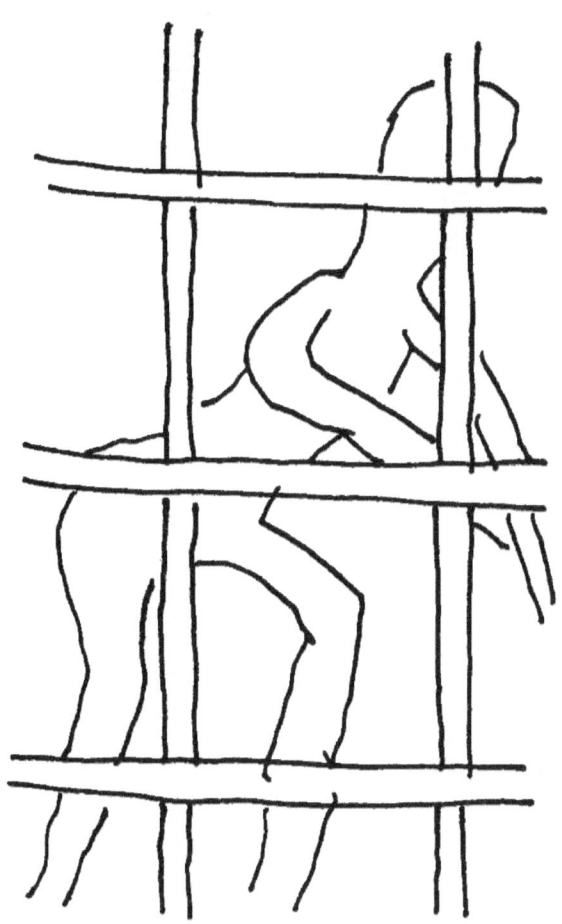

عابود الود يعة

عابود الود يعة
قريبة من رام اللهَّ
حيث يسوع نفسه
يوماً بشَّر عند كل باب

والآن يبني المستعمرون جداراً
ويسرقون ماءكم ويسمّمون
يوم السبت نفسه
عندما تفشل الأخلاق

هل يعتقدون أن الله غير موجود؟
أن دولتهم تخلّصها
أفران الماضي؟
أن جرائمهم تمحيها
الكذبة الإستعمارية؟
أن الحقيقة تظلَّ ساكتة
كما سكت الأطفال الذين قتلوهم؟

والآن جريمة التاريخ نفسها
تمحيها جريمتهم نفسها
وأرواح أهلهم
في خزي دائم

Gentle Aboud

Gentle Aboud

Just out from Ramallah

Where Jesus himself

Once preached at each door

Now the settlers build walls

Steal your water and poison

the Sabbath itself

As decency fails

Do they think there's no God?

That their State is redeemed

By the ovens of yore?

That their crimes are expunged

By colonial fiction?

That the truth will lie silent

As the children they've killed?

Now history's own crime

Is erased by their own

and the souls of their parents

in permanent shame

يئنون من خسارة

كل ما كان إنسانياً

مدمّر في قهر

الخير والسمعة

والآن جيش في شيلان الصلاة

هائجون في الكروم

كسروا أحلامنا

مدوسة ومنبوذة

مثل الزيتون والجداول.

إن الباقي الذي يسمى "المختار"

الآن متجمد، منبوذ،

سوف يكون محتقراً على مدى الزمان

في خيانة ربّهم

خرّبوا المفضلين عنده

الفلاحون الأبرياء

الذي حبّهم كأنه الطعام

البستان البريء

لعابود الود يعة

groan at the forfeit

all that was human

destroyed in the conquest

of goodness and name

Now an army in prayer shawls

Rampaging in orchards

Has broken our dreams

Bulldozed and discarded

Like the olives and streams.

The remnant called "chosen"

Now frozen, rejected,

Will be scorned for all time

In betraying their God

They've wasted his favorites

The innocent farmers

Whose love is as food

The innocent garden

Of Gentle Aboud

صفّقوا بأيديكم لفلسطين

بعض الناس يعلّمون الإسترضاء

للربّ القاسي والغيران

هو الذي قوانينه، في تخصيص صارم

بالرغم من صبّ النهر الداخلي،

يجب أن تتطبق تطبقاً دقيقاً

أم تقع النكبة وقوعا غير متقيد

ويتحطم الشعب

ويقُتل البقر

ويخُسرالأطفال

ويُكسرالكبار

مطحونون مثل القمح

في عجلة داخل عجلة داخل عجلة

كما يحتاج كل نكبة إلى شيء يحل محله

يحتاج إلى جدار

إستيقظوا

ويحتاج إلى الثأر

مثل الربّ ذي نوبة غضب

الذي يحرث الأرض

ليغلب الموت

من غيبوبة الترخيص الخاص

لوضع جدار

مؤسس على تألم سابق

Clap Hands For Palestine

some teach appeasement

of the hard and jealous god

a He whose rules, with rigid specificity

despite the inner river's flow,

must be followed closely

or disaster fall unleashed

the people crushed

the cattle slain

the children forfeit

elders broken

ground as grain

in a wheel inside a wheel inside a wheel

as each disaster needs replacement

needs a wall

wake up

needs blood revenge

like the Temper Tantrum God

who plows the land

to conquer death

from the trance of special license

to place a wall

based on suffering before

ومن خارجه

قد يحافظ البؤساء على

ما تبقى من الحياة نفسها

ليأكلوا التراب الذي ولدوا فيه أولاً

ليذوقوا جزمة أولاد أجانب

إستيقظوا ثانيا

في لهجات أمريكا

أوستراليا،

الأم روسيا

سوق البقر

حلقة المزارعين

مع أطفالهم

أمهاتهم، زوجاتهم،

عندما أصفّق بيديّ

نازلون منحدرات مصممة للغلة

للقمح ليطحن

إستيقظوا

أو مع ذلك بدلاً منه

قد نقرر أن ننقذ أرواحنا

ونقدم السلام

لا على طاولة يملأها ورق

ولكن على واحدة تطوف بالأكل والشراب

مزعجون من أصوات أطفال وهم يلعبون

فرحانة، أحلى مما سيعرفون حتى فيما بعد

outside of which

the wretched may preserve

what remains of life itself

to eat the dirt they first were born in

to taste the boot of foreign boys

wake up again

in accents of America

Australia,

Mother Russia

cattle drive

the circle of the farmers

with their children

mothers, wives,

when I clap my hands

down ramps designed for produce

for wheat to grind

wake up

or still, instead

we could decide to save our souls

and offer peace

not at a table filled with paper

but one which groans with food and drink

disturbed by children's playsounds

happy, sweeter than they'll know till later

وقدمت الشفقة الإنسانية أيضاً،

مثل سلام الإعتراف صفقوا إبتهاج

ويطالب هذا بنهاية للقتل،

التطهير العرقي الإبادة الجماعية

بالضبط الشيء الذي بدأنا

على هذه الركبة الغيورة الحاكمة.

human kindness also served,

as peace of recognition *clap* delight

and this demands an end to murder,

ethnic cleansing genocide

just the thing that got us started

on this jealous ruling ride.

هل تريد أن تناقش إذا هذه إبادة جماعية أم لا؟

فلننسى التعبير نسياناً كلياً

فهو تعبير صنعي معاصر

لما فعله القبائل منذ قبل قبل

إخترعه رافائيل لامكين

1943

لتسمية ما كان يحدث لنا

وما حتى ذلك الوقت

كان يعرف بجريمة الهمجية

والآن بلإبادة الجماعية

التي أعرف أني

ولكنها فُعلت فينا نحن

والآن نفعلها نحن في شخص آخر

والآن نعملها نحن في الشخص الثاني

الفلسطينيون

إذا يسمح لنا ذلك التعبير

مثل كلمة "اليهودي" أو بالأحرى، "يودين"

كلمة كانت من المفروض أنها إنمحت

معنا

ولم تنمحي

ولكن حياتنا

ألف عام في أوربا

You Want to Quibble Over Whether or Not It's Genocide?

Then let's forget the word entirely

it's a made up modern word

for what's been done by tribes since before before

made up by Raphael Lemkin

1943

to name what was happening to us

which until then

was known as the crime of barbarity

now genocide

which I know

I agreed not to mention

but it was done to us

and now we're doing it to the next guy

the Palestinians

if we are allowed that word

like the word 'Jew' or really, "Juden"

a word that was supposed to be wiped out

with us

but wasn't

but our lives

one thousand years in Europe

وطننا، مطهّر منّا

وقالوا إننا لم نكن شعباً حقيقياً

"شعب طبقة" قال لينين

"مرض" قال آخرون

والآن نعمله نحن في الشخص الثاني

طيب، لا أفران الغاز

ما نعرف عنها بعد

ولكن غازات سامة بكثرة

غرف للتعذيب

نوع خاص للتعليق يسمّى "التعليق الفلسطيني"

الذي يستعمله الأمريكيون الآن

يعلق إنسان

من معصميه

مربوطين معاً

لتحت ومن وراء

إلى أن يعصروا رئاتهم بأنفسهم

على ساعات

ويمكن بعض الأيام

ويموتوا موتاً مرعباً

ويستعمل كثيراً

حتى يسمى "تعليق فلسطيني"

وإسرقوا الأرض

وحوّطوهم بجدار

وجوّعوا أطفالهم

our home, cleansed of us

and they said we were not a true people

"a people class" said Lenin

"a disease" said others

and now we're doing it to the next guy

OK, no gas ovens

that we know of yet

but poison gas aplenty

torture rooms

a special hanging called "a Palestinian hanging"

that now the Americans use

hang a human

by the wrists

tied together

back behind

till they crush their own lungs

over hours

maybe a few days

and die in horror

done so much

it's called "a Palestinian hanging"

and steal the land

and wall them in

and starve their babies

إضربوا الحوامل أمام أطفالهن

أمهاتهن

أزواجهن

والأرض، سارقونها، محوّطونها، ساحجون عليها،

ماحيون أسماء الأماكن.

لا أقدر أن أجد قرية جدتي

على خريطة بيلاروس، هي التي سمّتها "روسيا البيضاء."

سمّيت "كابوليا،" و"قرب مينسك،"

ولكنها ليست هناك،

كما ليست هناك فلسطين.

beat the pregnant women in front of their children

their mothers

their husbands

and the land, stealing it, walling it, pissing on it,

wiping out the place names.

I can't find my grandmother's village

on a map of Belarus, what she called "White Russia."

It was called "Kapulya," "near Minsk,"

but it's not there.

as isn't Palestine.

يا ! فلسطين!

يا! فلسطين!

لم أسمع إسمك أبداً

بل سميتك إسرائيل

وعرفت أنك كنت لِيّ للإستيلاء

من حيث أتى أهلي

والآن يرجعون، معي، للإستعمار

ولكن عندما رأيت تلالك

شعرت جديداً مثل سيسيل رودز

مثل كورتيز وكولومبوس

مثل ساميويل دي شامبلين

قابلت أنبل شيوخك

أطلقت النار عليهم فماتوا وهم حاملون هدايا

ذرة للمشاركة

ولحم وجلد

ذبحت أحسنكم

وأجوّعك جوعاً منذ ذلك الوقت

ولا أسمح لك

أن تدفني موتاك

ولا تغذي مرضاك

ولا ترضعي صغارك

ولا تحفري أرضك

ولا تباركيها إلى الخصوبة

O! Palestine!

O! Palestine!

I never heard your name

I called you Israel

and knew that you were mine to claim

from whence my people came

and now return, with me, to settle

But as I saw your hills

I felt as new as Cecil Rhodes

As Cortez and Columbus

Like Samuel DeChamplain

I met your noblest chieftains

I shot them dead as they bore gifts

of corn to share

and meat and skins

I slew your best

and starve you since

and suffer you not

to bury your dead

nor feed your sick

to nurse the young

nor scratch your earth

and bless it to fecundity

بل أغلب حتى الكلمات
وأغيّر إسم الحقل والبلد
لكي من يتطوف منكم
لا يستطيع أن يجد موطنه
لن يكون له موطناً

I conquer even words

and change the name of field and town

so those of you who wander

cannot find home

are never home

إلى أشرف أبي رحمة

الكلمة من أربعة حروف (بالإنجليزية) والتي تبدأ بصوت ال"ن"

لا يسمح لنا البعض أن نقولها

(والحرف الثالث هو ال "ز")

ولكن هل يسمح لنا أن نقول مي لاي؟

أو كينت ستيت أو آتيكا؟

أو بابي يار أو لفوف؟

فلنتحدث عن ساند كريك

"درب الدموع"، كريزي هورس،

الذي يدعى

تاشونكيويتكو

ممسوك بلا حركة بحراسه

بلطجية دفعوا لهم

المستعمرون وأصحاب البنوك

متمدد مثل الفريسة

كان مسلسلاً

عاجزاً ومقيداً

في نيبراسكا

حصن روبينسون

وحصدوه وهو واقفاً

متعذبا ممسوكا

مثل الفتى في نعلين

أشرف أبو رحمة

For Ashraf Abu Rahmeh

the four-letter n-word

we're not allowed by some to say

(third letter Z)

but may we say My-Lai?

or Kent State or Attica

Babi-Yar or Lvov ?

Then let's speak of Sand Creek

Trail of Tears, Crazy Horse,

who was called

Tashunkewitko

held still by his guards

thugs in the pay

of the settlers and bankers

splayed out like prey

in chains he was

helpless and bound

in Nebraska

Fort Robinson

cut down as he stood

tormented and held

like the boy in Nil'in

Ashraf Abu Rahmeh

الذي كان ملزم اليدين من جنديين إسرائيل،

مقيد اليدين ومحتجزا،

معصوب العينين، مكبوحا

ومصابا برصاصة في رجله أطلقت عليه بلا رحمة

وعن قرب

فقط لأنه صاح صيحة عالية

على جنود إسرائيل

"كفى هذا العنف!"

في مظاهرة غاندية

لمقاومة سلمية

على جدار يعتبر غير قانوني

بل يعتبر قاسياً ويعتبر سرقة،

في قرية في فلسطين، نعلين،

في الضفة الغربية

في المزقة الباقية من فلسطين،

محروقة إلى رماد تقريباً

ولكن لا يزال قلبها مثمراً،

تلمع لمعاً أخضر مثل الزيتون الطازج

سلسلة الأسلاف تمتد أحمر

على الرمل البلوري الأبيض

كما يقترب الدخان المسوّد

لبيت الموق

ولا يزال ممنوعاً

أننا نذكر تعبير الإبادة الجماعية

who was held by his arms, by two soldiers of Israel

handcuffed and held,

blindfolded, restrained

coldly shot in the leg

at close range

just for shouting out loud

at the soldiers of Israel

"enough with this violence!"

at a Gandhian protest

of peaceful resistance

to a wall deemed illegal

deemed cruel and deemed theft,

in a village in Palestine, Ni'lin,

in West Bank

in the shred left of Palestine,

near burnt to a cinder

with a heart still so fruitful,

it shines green like fresh olives

and a bloodline runs red

on the crystal white sand

as the blackening smoke

of the charnel house nears

and still prohibition

of mentioning genocide

الإبادة الجماعية تطحن

ويُفنى شعب

وحبنا لحياتهم

يمحا من قلوبنا

عن طريق حملة حقد

وكلام مزيف عن حق المولد

جنّ الدين جنونه

أو مجرد الإقتصاد

من يجب أن يموت لثروة من؟

كما نتبع المال

دائماً يرجع إلى قاعدته

دائماً يرجع إلى قاعدته.

and the genocide grinds

and a people expire

as our love for their lives

is expunged from our hearts

through a campaign of hatred

and false talk of birthright

religion run wild

or just economics

who must die for whose purse?

as we follow the money

it always comes home

it always comes home.

يوم الإثنين في فلسطين

ينتهي الطعام

والسجون تحترق

تدخل قوات إسرائيلية

تخترق جرافة مخيّماً

ولم يرحم الوسط

أجزاء معدن ملتوية

وقد قتل خمسة أشخاص

"ضربنا الضربة"

وجُرح بعض الآخرون

يبيع الرجل فولاً لعمله

بينما الولد الذي عمره عشر سنوات

كان في المنطقة بكل بساطة

عائش يوم الإثنين صباحاً

حين هاجم الجنود

وفتّشوا،

حاجزون الأطفال

ودخلوا العيادة

وبالوا على الأرض

أعتقلت أختان

وقال الأب إن لم تكن لإبنتيه

أفكاراً سياسية

رانية ورامية

Palestine Monday

running out of food

the prisons are on fire

Israeli forces penetrate

bulldozer breaks through camp

the center was not spared

twisted bits of metal

Five people have been killed

"We carried out a strike"

several more were injured

The man sells beans for work

while the 10 year old

was simply in the area

living Monday morning

when soldiers made attack

and searched,

detaining children

they came into the clinic

urinated on the floor

two sisters were arrested

the father said his daughters

had no political ideas

Ranya and Ramya

كانتا تعملان

في مشغل خياطة

في قرية حوّارة

يسوق والدهما سيارة أجرة

وقد أعتقلت الفتاتان الآن

وموقعهما غير معروف

have been working

in a sewing workshop

in the village of Huwwarah

their father drives a taxi

now the girls have been arrested

their location is unknown

فلتسمعي يا إسرائيل إن أهل غزة لبشر!

ماهي طقوس إباحة الدم الهمجية؟

هل هذا هو النعيم؟ هل هو التطهير الروحي؟

أهي مراسم البشرية لإنشاء مستعمرة ؟

قتل الأطفال و أمهاتهم

الاعتداء على سجناء لا حول لهم أو قوة

قتل الأسرى في أقفاصهم

والتقدم حسب التعليمات

مُلوِّحين بأعلام بيضاء

وتطلب منشوراتهم

التحرك نحو مدرسة:

من أجل أمنكم

حسب التعليمات

توجهوا نحو المدرسة

إلى العدو المجابه

وجابهوا الأطفال فقط

الذين يرمي أعمامهم و أخوالهم و آباءهم من هنا و هناك

حجارة وشمعُ رومانياً

فيُردي الجنود الأم والأخت و ذو الخمسة أعوام

برصاصة في الرأس، برأس الطفل

أكثر من طفل

وأكثر من رصاصة ... في رأس كل طفل

ويتكرر هذا اليوم في أخبارنا يومياً

Hear, O Israel: Gaza is Human!

What is this ritual of savage bloodletting?

Is this the bris? the circumcision?

manhood ceremony for a colony?

this shooting of children and their mothers

assault on helpless prisoners

killing of captives in their cage

advancing as instructed

waving white flags

as the pamphlet ordered

moving toward the school

to be safe

as instructed

moving toward the school

as the opposing army

opposing only children

with their rag-tag dads and uncles

hurling stones and Roman candles

soldier shoots down mother, sister, five-year-old

puts bullets in their heads, the children

more than one child

more than one bullet per child's head

repeated this day on NPR

لابد أن الوقت كان في حوالي الثالثة ظهراً

حين ضعُف إيماننا

وتحطمت قلوبنا

وتلاشت آمالنا

بانتصار إسرائيل ثانيةً على الأطفال

غير مسلّحين

متبررين فلسطين

في الرابع عشر من يناير

عام ألفين وتسعة.

ترجمة: أ. ريم الدخيل

it must have been about 3pm

that our faith was broken

hearts shattered

hope demolished

Israel triumphs again over children

the unarmed

the justified of Palestine

January Fourteenth

two thousand nine.

Translated into Arabic by A. Reem Aldakheel

إنهم يجعلونا نشعر كأننا لا شيء

"إنهم يجعلونا نشعر كأننا لا شيء.

إنهم يجعلونا نشعر أننا لا شيء.

ويعاملونا كأننا لا شيء؛

ويعاملونا كأننا حيوانات،"

قالت الطفلة الصغيرة من غزة.

"لا، هذا غلط."

هي واضحة ومأدّبة قوية في غضبها.

"يعاملونا معاملة أسوأ مما يعاملون الحيوانات."

وهي أحدّ في خيبة آمالها

مما يقدر أن يكون الشخص وحليب الأم يصبّ،

غير مستعجل، في السلامة، في البيت،

حين تكون الكتب مفتوحة، والمدرسة ممتعة.

هي حزينة، وتدقّق:

"أنهم يحبّون الحيوانات أكثر كثيراً مما يحبّونا،

فيعاملونا كأننا لا شيء، ويجعلنا

نشعر أنا لسنا من البشر."

وهي صغيرة لعمرها.

أربعة عشر عاما تقريباً.

فتاة.

متعلمة.

They Make Us Feel Like We Are Nothing

"They make us feel like we are nothing.

They make us feel that we are nothing.

They treat us like we are nothing;

they treat us like we are animals,"

said the little girl from Gaza.

"No, that is wrong,"

She is clear and fiercely polite in her anger.

"They treat us worse than they treat animals,"

She is sharper in disappointment

than one can be when mother's milk is flowing,

unhurried, in safety, at home,

when books are open, and school is fun.

She is sad, and is being precise:

"they care much more for animals than they do for us,

so they treat us like we are nothing, and it makes us

feel that we are not a part of people."

She is small for her age.

About fourteen.

A young woman.

Educated.

محاولة أن تركّز على المدرسة،

تعتني بأخواتها.

وتعاني أمهن من السرطان،

إمرأة من غزة،

ولا يسمح لها أن تذهب إلى أبعد من مجموعة الزنزانات التي هي غزة لتحصل على المعالجة للسرطان.

وتظهر أن عندها حوالي إثنتان وثلاثين عاماً،

الأم،

التي تعاني من السرطان،

والتي لا يسمح لها أن تذهب إلى المستشفى خارج غزة

حيث يمكن أن يعالجوها بالمواد الكيميائية.

حيث الأطباء،

الذين ليسوا حيوانات،

يعرفون أنها من البشر،

ويودّون أنها تعيش.

ولكن في غزة تقدر أن تحصل على المورفين كل يوم لآلامها.

وقريباً ستموت، يقول طبيبها.

تقول إبنتها "نتأسف لها."

Trying to focus on school,

take care of her sisters.

Their mother has cancer,

a woman of Gaza,

and she is not allowed to go beyond

Cell Block Gaza

To get cancer treatment.

She looks about thirty-two,

the mother,

who has cancer,

and is not allowed to go to the hospital

outside of Gaza

where they could give her chemotherapy.

Where the doctors,

who are not animals,

know she is human,

and would like her to live.

But in Gaza she can get morphine

every day for her pain.

Soon she will die, says her doctor.

Her daughter says "We feel sorry for her."

لا تسرقوا

لا تسرقوا القدس

(أورشليم عندكم)

فمع أنكم تدّعون شيئاً

ليس حقيقياً

إستردّوا، بدلها،

الأرض التي جاء أهلنا منها:

ليفوف وبابي يار

(لتقل الإسم).

وبولندة، أعيدوا بلونسك

وستانيسلاوف، موطننا؛

يا رومانيا إدخليني

عندي حقول أريد أن أزرعها

خارج تشيرنوفيتز.

وإلى اليوم،

في بوكوفينا،

قريباً من سوتشافا،

تقف مطحنة يجريها الماء:

هذه الحنطة حقيقية،

وطحينها لي،

Steal Not

Steal not Al-Quds

(Jerusalem to you)

For though you make a claim

It isn't true

Take back, instead,

the land from where our parents came:

Lvov and Babi Yar

(to say the name).

And Poland, give back Plonsk

And Stanislaw, our home;

Romania, let me in

I have some fields to plant

outside of Czernowitz.

And still,

In Bukovina,

close to Suczawa,

there stands a water-driven mill:

This grist is real,

its flour mine,

ولكن يجب ألاّ يقع

بيت آخر

في فلسطين

but not another house

must fall

In Palestine

Translator's Note

When Marc Estrin and Bob Green invited me, with the assistance of my husband Mousa Ishaq, to participate in this project by translating Bob's poems into Arabic, I found myself unable to refuse. This may sound ungracious, but it is true for several reasons.

First, Bob Green's poetry is deeply personal and experiential. It speaks directly to every reader, penetrating deep within one's very heart. Deceptively simple at times, it makes use of homely metaphors—an ant on a kitchen counter, the scent of lemons and limes—occasional humor, and powerful imagery to drive home the unpleasant facts of the Israeli occupation. At other times, the poet's voice is lyrical, singing the song of exile and its burden for both the Jewish and Palestinian peoples—for all peoples. Indeed, Bob Green's universalist sensibility—his capacity to understand and articulate the oppressor's thoughts and feelings as well as those of the oppressed—sets his poetry apart. Born into a family with deep Zionist connections yet imbued with the highest traditions of ethical Judaism, he has found himself grappling with the essential paradox of the Israeli colonial enterprise: How can one demand rights for oneself while denying those same rights to the other? This question permeates his poetry, at times forcefully and at other times sorrowfully, but it is ever present.

Second, such poetry needs to be accessible to as many people as possible. It is our hope that those who read the poetry in Arabic will themselves become part of a wider circle, one in which mutual understanding and the bonds of our common humanity hold sway. If the translation that accompanies Bob Green's poetry helps in any way to achieve this aim, we will be well satisfied.

Finally, we would be remiss if Mousa and I did not acknowledge our deep and decades-long friendship with Bob, which extends to our families and unites us with strong bonds of love and respect. "Just Lemons and Limes" was written about Mousa's mother, "Auntie Salma," as she lay dying with her family and closest friends, including Bob, around her. "Gentle Aboud" describes the village where Mousa was born and the home of his fondest memories, a place that Bob has not yet visited but one to which we all hope to travel together one day. And one day Palestinians and Israelis will be free from the occupation that has poisoned their souls—free to embrace their common humanity. It is our fervent belief that the beauty, insight, and power of Bob Green's poetry will hasten the advent of that day.

–Kristin Peterson-Ishaq

Fomite
Burlington, Vermont

A fomite is a medium capable of transmitting infectious organisms from one individual to another.

"The activity of art is based on the capacity of people to be infected by the feelings of others." Tolstoy, *What Is Art?*

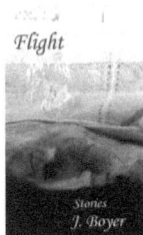

Flight and Other Stories - Jay Boyer
In *Flight and Other Stories,* we're with the fattest woman on earth as she draws her last breaths and her soul ascends toward its final reward. We meet a divorcee who can fly with no more effort than flapping her arms. We follow a middle-aged butler whose love affair with a young woman leads him first to the mysteries of bondage and then to the pleasures of malice. Story by story, we set foot into worlds so strange as to seem all but surreal, yet everything feels familiar, each moment rings true. And that's when we recognize we're in the hands of one of America's truly original talents.

Loisaida - Dan Chodorokoff
Catherine, a young anarchist estranged from her parents and squatting in an abandoned building on New York's Lower East Side, is fighting with her boyfriend and conflicted about her work on an underground newspaper. After learning of a developer's plans to demolish a community garden, Catherine builds an alliance with a group of Puerto Rican community activists. Together they confront the confluence of politics, money, and real estate that rule Manhattan. All the while she learns important lessons from her great-grandmother's life in the Yiddish anarchist movement that flourished on the Lower East Side at the turn of the century. In this coming-of-age story, family saga, and tale of urban politics, Dan Chodorkoff explores the "principle of hope" and examines how memory and imagination inform social change.

Improvisational Arguments - Anna Faktorovich
Improvisational Arguments is written in free verse to capture the essence of modern problems and triumphs. The poems clearly relate short, frequently humorous, and occasionally tragic stories about travels to exotic and unusual places, fantastic realms, abnormal jobs, artistic innovations, political objections, and misadventures with love.

Carts and Other Stories - Zdravka Evtimova
Roots and wings are the key words that best describe the short story collection *Carts and Other Stories,* by Zdravka Evtimova. The book is emotionally multilayered and memorable because of its internal power, vitality and ability to touch both your heart and your mind. Within its pages, the reader discovers new perspectives and true wealth, and learns to see the world with different eyes. The collection lives on the borders of different cultures. *Carts and Other Stories* will take the reader to wild and powerful Bulgarian mountains, to silver rains in Brussels, to German quiet winter streets, and to wind-bitten crags in Afghanistan. This book lives for those seeking to discover the beauty of the world around them, and will have them appreciating what they have—and perhaps what they have lost as well.

Fomite
Burlington, Vermont

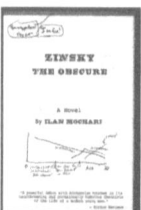

Zinsky the Obscure - Ilan Mochari
"If your childhood is brutal, your adulthood becomes a daily attempt to recover: a quest for ecstasy and stability in recompense for their early absence." So states the 30-year-old Ariel Zinsky, whose bachelor-like lifestyle belies the torturous youth he is still coming to grips with. As a boy, he struggles with the beatings themselves; as a grownup, he struggles with the world's indifference to them. Zinsky the Obscure is his life story, a humorous chronicle of his search for a redemptive ecstasy through sex, an entrepreneurial sports obsession, and finally, the cathartic exercise of writing it all down. Fervently recounting both the comic delights and the frightening horrors of a life in which he feels—always—that he is not like all the rest, Zinsky survives the worst and relishes the best with idiosyncratic style, as his heartbreak turns into self-awareness and his suicidal ideation into self-regard. A vivid evocation of the all-consuming nature of lust and ambition—and the forces that drive them.

Kasper Planet: Comix and Tragix - Peter Schumann
The British call him Punch; the Italians, Pulchinella; the Russians, Petruchka; the Native Americans, Coyote. These are the figures we may know. But every culture that worships authority will breed a Punch-like, anti-authoritarian resister. Yin and yang—it has to happen. The Germans call him Kasper. Truth-telling and serious pranking are dangerous professions when going up against power. Bradley Manning sits naked in solitary; Julian Assange is pursued by Interpol, Obama's Department of Justice, and Amazon.com. But—in contrast to merely human faces— masks and theater can often slip through the bars. Consider our American Kaspers: Charlie Chaplin, Woody Guthrie, Abby Hoffman, the Yes Men—theater people all, utilizing various forms to seed critique. Their profiles and tactics have evolved along with those of their enemies. Who are the bad guys that call forth the Kaspers? Over the last half century, with his Bread & Puppet Theater, Peter Schumann has been tireless in naming them, excoriating them with Kasperdom....
from Marc Estrin's Foreword to Planet Kasper

The Co-Conspirator's Tale - Ron Jacobs
There's a place where love and mistrust are never at peace; where duplicity and deceit are the universal currency. The Co-Conspirator's Tale takes place within this nebulous firmament. There are crimes committed by the police in the name of the law. Excess in the name of revolution. The combination leaves death in its wake and the survivors struggling to find justice in a San Francisco Bay Area noir by the author of the underground classic The Way the Wind Blew: A History of the Weather Underground and the novel Short Order Frame Up.

Short Order Frame Up - Ron Jacobs
1975. America as lost its war in Vietnam and Cambodia. Racially tinged riots are tearing the city of Boston apart. The politics and counterculture of the 1960s are disintegrating into nothing more than sex, drugs, and rock and roll. The Boston Red Sox are on one of their improbable runs toward a postseason appearance. In a suburban town in Maryland, a young couple are murdered and another young man is accused. The couple are white and the accused is black. It is up to his friends and family to prove he is innocent. This is a story of suburban ennui, race, murder, and injustice. Religion and politics, liberal lawyers and racist cops. In Short Order Frame Up, Ron Jacobs has written a piece of crime fiction that exposes the wound that is US racism. Two cultures existing side by side and across generations--a river very few dare to cross. His characters work and live with and next to each other, often unaware of each other's real life. When the murder occurs, however, those people that care about the man charged must cross that river and meet somewhere in between in order to free him from (what is to them) an obvious miscarriage of justice.

Fomite
Burlington, Vermont

All the Sinners Saints - Ron Jacobs
A young draftee named Victor Willard goes AWOL in Germany after an altercation with a commanding officer. Porgy is an African-American GI involved with the international Black Panthers and German radicals. Victor and a female radical named Ana fall in love. They move into Ana's room in a squatted building near the US base in Frankfurt. The international campaign to free Black revolutionary Angela Davis is coming to Frankfurt. Porgy and Ana are key organizers and Victor spends his days and nights selling and smoking hashish, while becoming addicted to heroin. Police and narcotics agents are keeping tabs on them all. Politics, love, and drugs. Truths, lies, and rock and roll. *All the Sinners Saints* is a story of people seeking redemption in a world awash in sin.

Loosestrife - Greg Delanty
This book is a chronicle of complicity in our modern lives, a witnessing of war and the destruction of our planet. It is also an attempt to adjust the more destructive blueprint myths of our society. Often our cultural memory tells us to keep quiet about the aspects that are most challenging to our ethics, to forget the violations we feel and tremors that keep us distant and numb.

Roadworthy Creature, Roadworthy Craft - Kate Magill
Words fail but the voice struggles on. The culmination of a decade's worth of performance poetry, *Roadworthy Creature, Roadworthy Craft* is Kate Magill's first full-length publication. In lines that are sinewy yet delicate, Magill's poems explore the terrain where idea and action meet, where bodies and words commingle to form a strange new flesh, a breathing text, an "I" that spirals outward from itself.

The Listener Aspires to the Condition of Music - Barry Goldensohn
"I know of no other selected poems that selects on one theme, but this one does, charting Goldensohn's career-long attraction to music's performance, consolations and its august, thrilling, scary and clownish charms. Does all art aspire to the condition of music as Pater claimed, exhaling in a swoon toward that one class act? Goldensohn is more aware than the late 19th century of the overtones of such breathing: his poems thoroughly round out those overtones in a poet's lifetime of listening." John Peck, poet, editor, Fellow of the American Academy of Rome

The Derivation of Cowboys & Indians - Joseph D. Reich
The Derivation of Cowboys & Indians represents a profound journey, a breakdown of the American Dream from a social, cultural, historical, and spiritual point of view. Reich examines in concise detail the loss of the collective unconscious, commenting on our contemporary postmodern culture with its self-interested excesses, on where and how things all go wrong, and how social/political practice rarely meets its original proclamations and promises. Reich's surreal and self-effacing satire brings this troubling message home. *The Derivation of Cowboys & Indians* is a desperate search and struggle for America's literal, symbolic, and spiritual home.

Fomite
Burlington, Vermont

Views Cost Extra - L.E. Smith

Views that inspire, that calm, or that terrify—all come at some cost to the viewer. In *Views Cost Extra* you will find a New Jersey high school preppy who wants to inhabit the "perfect" cowboy movie, a rural mailman disgusted with the residents of his town who wants to live with the penguins, an ailing screen-writer who strikes a deal with Johnny Cash to reverse an old man's failures, an old man who ponders a young man's suicide attempt, a one-armed blind blues singer who wants to reunite with the car that took her arm on the assembly line— and more. These stories suggest that we must pay something to live even ordinary lives.

The Empty Notebook Interrogates Itself - Susan Thomas

The Empty Notebook began its life as a very literal metaphor for a few weeks of what the poet thought was writer's block, but was really the struggle of an eccentric persona to take over her working life. It won. And for the next three years everything she wrote came to her in the voice of the Empty Notebook, who, as the notebook began to fill itself, became rather opinionated, changed gender, alternately acted as bully and victim, had many bizarre adventures in exotic locales, and developed a somewhat politically incorrect attitude. It then began to steal the voices and forms of other poets and tried to immortalize itself in various poetry reviews. It is now thrilled to collect itself in one slim volume.

My God, What Have We Done? - Susan Weiss

In a world afflicted with war, toxicity, and hunger, does what we do in our private lives really matter? Fifty years after the creation of the atomic bomb at Los Alamos, newlyweds Pauline and Clifford visit that once-secret city on their honeymoon, compelled by Pauline's fascination with Oppenheimer, the soulful scientist. The two stories emerging from this visit reverberate back and forth between the loneliness of a new mother at home in Boston and the isolation of an entire community dedicated to the development of the bomb. While Pauline struggles with unforeseen challenges of family life, Oppenheimer and his crew reckon with forces beyond all imagining. Finally the years of frantic research on the bomb culminate in a stunning test explosion that echoes a rupture in the couple's marriage. Against the backdrop of a civilization that's out of control, Pauline begins to understand the complex, potentially explosive physics of personal relationships. At once funny and dead serious, *My God, What Have We Done?* sifts through the ruins left by the bomb in search of a more worthy human achievement.

Visiting Hours - Jennifer Anne Moses

Visiting Hours, a novel-in-stories, explores the lives of people not normally met on the page—-AIDS patients and those who care for them. Set in Baton Rouge, Louisiana, and written with large and frequent dollops of humor, the book is a profound meditation on faith and love in the face of illness and poverty.

Raven or Crow - Joshua Amses

Marlowe has recently moved back home to Vermont after flunking his first term at a private college in the Midwest, when his sort-of girlfriend, Eleanor, goes missing. The circumstances surrounding Eleanor's disappearance stand to reveal more about Marlowe than he is willing to allow. Rather than report her missing, he resolves to find Eleanor himself. *Raven or Crow* is the story of mistakes rooted in the ambivalence of being young and without direction.

Fomite
Burlington, Vermont

As It Is On Earth - Peter M. Wheelwright
Four centuries after the Reformation Pilgrims sailed up the down-flowing watersheds of New England, Taylor Thatcher, irreverent scion of a fallen family of Maine Puritans, is still caught in the turbulence. In his errant attempts to escape from history, the young college professor is further unsettled by his growing attraction to Israeli student Miryam Bluehm as he is swept by Time through the "family thing"—from the tangled genetic and religious history of his New England parents to the redemptive birthday secret of Esther Fleur Noire Bishop, the Cajun-Passamaquoddy woman who raised him and his younger half-cousin/half-brother, Bingham.The landscapes, rivers, and tidal estuaries of Old New England and the Mayan Yucatan are also casualties of history in Thatcher's story of Deep Time and re-discovery of family on Columbus Day at a high-stakes gambling casino, rising in resurrection over the starlit bones of a once-vanquished Pequot Indian tribe.

Suite for Three Voices - Derek Furr
Suite for Three Voices is a dance of prose genres, teeming with intense human life in all its humor and sorrow. A son uncovers the horrors of his father's wartime experience, a hitchhiker in a muumuu guards a mysterious parcel, a young man foresees his brother's brush with death on September 11. A Victorian poetess encounters space aliens and digital archives, a runner hears the voice of a dead friend in the song of an indigo bunting, a teacher seeks wisdom from his students' errors and Neil Young. By frozen waterfalls and neglected graveyards, along highways at noon and rivers at dusk, in the sound of bluegrass, Beethoven, and Emily Dickinson, the essays and fiction in this collection offer moments of vision.

Travers' Inferno - L.E. Smith
In the 1970's, churches began to burn in Burlington, Vermont. If it was arson, no one or no reason could be found to blame. This book suggests arson, but makes no claim to historical realism. It claims, instead, to capture the dizzying 70's zeitgeist of aggressive utopian movements, distrust in authority, escapist alternative lifestyles, and a bewildered society of onlookers. In the tradition of John Gardner's *Sunlight Dialogues*, the characters of *Travers' Inferno* are colorful and damaged, sometimes comical, sometimes tragic, looking for meaning through desperate acts. Travers Jones, the protagonist, is grounded in the transcendent—philosophy, epilepsy, arson as purification— and mystified by the opposite sex, haunted by an absent father and directed by an uncle with a grudge. He is seduced by a professor's wife and chased by an endearing if ineffective sergeant of police. There are secessionist Quebecois involved in these church burns who are murdering as well as pilfering and burning. There are changing alliances, violent deaths, lovemaking, and a belligerent cat.

Still Time - Michael Cocchiarale
Still Time is a collection of twenty-five short and shorter stories exploring tensions that arise in a variety of contemporary relationships: a young boy must deal with the wrath of his out-of-work father; a woman runs into a man twenty years after an awkward sexual encounter; a wife, unable to conceive, imagines her own murder, as well as the reaction of her emotionally distant husband; a soon-to-be-tenured English professor tries to come to terms with her husband's shocking return to the religion of his youth; an assembly line worker, married for thirty years, discovers the surprising secret life of his recently hospitalized wife. Whether a few hundred or a few thousand words, these and other stories in the collection depict characters at moments of deep crisis. Some feel powerless, overwhelmed—unable to do much to change the course of their lives. Others rise to the occasion and, for better or for worse, say or do the thing that might transform them for good. Even in stories with the most troubling of endings, there remains the possibility of redemption. For each of the characters, there is still time.

Fomite
Burlington, Vermont

The Housing Market - Joseph D. Reich

In Joseph Reich's most recent social and cultural, contemporary satire of suburbia entitled, "The Housing market: a comfortable place to jump off the end of the world," the author addresses the absurd, postmodern elements of what it means, or for that matter not, to try and cope and function, and survive and thrive, or live and die in the repetitive and existential, futile and self-destructive, homogenized, monochromatic landscape of a brutal and bland, collective unconscious, which can spiritually result in a gradual wasting away and erosion of the senses or conflict and crisis of a desperate, disproportionate 'situational depression,' triggering and leading the narrator to feel constantly abandoned and stranded, more concretely or proverbially spoken, "the eternal stranger," where when caught between the fight or flight psychological phenomena, naturally repels him and causes him to flee and return without him even knowing it into the wild, while by sudden circumstance and coincidence discovers it surrounds the illusory-like circumference of these selfsame Monopoly board cul-de-sacs and dead ends. Most specifically, what can happen to a solitary, thoughtful, and independent thinker when being stagnated in the triangulation of a cookie-cutter, oppressive culture of a homeowner's association; a memoir all written in critical and didactic, poetic stanzas and passages, and out of desperation, when freedom and control get taken, what he is forced to do in the illusion of 'free will and volition,' something like the derivative art of a smart and ironic and social and cultural satire.

Signed Confessions - Tom Walker

Guilt and a desperate need to repent drive the antiheroes in Tom Walker's dark (and often darkly funny) stories:
A gullible journalist falls for the 40-year-old stripper he profiles in a magazine.
A faithless husband abandons his family and joins a support group for lost souls.
A merciless prosecuting attorney grapples with the suicide of his gay son.
An aging misanthrope must make amends to five former victims.
An egoistic naval hero is haunted by apparitions of his dead wife and a mysterious little girl.
The seven tales in *Signed Confessions* measure how far guilty men will go to obtain a forgiveness no one can grant but themselves.

Love's Labours - Jack Pulaski

In the four stories and two novellas that comprise *Love's Labors* the protagonists, Ben and Laura, discover in their fervid romance and long marriage their interlocking fates, and the histories that preceded their births. They also learned something of the paradox between love and all the things it brings to its beneficiaries: bliss, disaster, duty, tragedy, comedy, the grotesque, and tenderness. Ben and Laura's story is also the particularly American tale of immigration to a new world. Laura's story begins in Puerto Rico, and Ben's lineage is Russian-Jewish. They meet in City College of New York, a place at least analogous to a melting pot. Laura struggles to rescue her brother from gang life and heroin. She is mother to her younger sister; their mother Consuelo is the financial mainstay of the family and consumed by work. Despite filial obligations, Laura aspires to be a serious painter. Ben writes, cares for, and is caught up in the misadventures and surreal stories of his younger schizophrenic brother. Laura is also a story teller as powerful and enchanting as Scheherazade. Ben struggles to survive such riches, and he and Laura endure.

Fomite
Burlington, Vermont

The Good Muslim of Jackson Heights - Jaysinh Birjépatil
Jackson Heights in this book is a fictional locale with common features assembled from immigrant-friendly neighborhoods around the world where hardworking honest-to-goodness traders from the Indian subcontinent rub shoulders with ruthless entrepreneurs, reclusive antique-dealers, homeless nobodies, merchant-princes, lawyers, doctors, and IT specialists. But as Siraj and Shabnam, urbane newcomers fleeing religious persecution in their homeland, discover, there is no escape from the past. Weaving together the personal and the political. *The Good Muslim of Jackson Heights* is an ambiguous elegy to a utopian ideal set free from all prejudice.

Meanwell - Janice Miller Potter
Meanwell is a twenty-four-poem sequence in which a female servant searches for identity and meaning in the shadow of her mistress, poet Anne Bradstreet. Although Meanwell herself is a fiction, someone like her could easily have existed among Bradstreet's known but unnamed domestic servants. Through Meanwell's eyes, Bradstreet emerges as a human figure during the Great Migration of the 1600s, a period in which the Massachusetts Bay Colony was fraught with physical and political dangers. Through Meanwell, the feelings of women, silenced during the midwife Anne Hutchinson's fiery trial before the Puritan ministers, are finally acknowledged. In effect, the poems are about the making of an American rebel. Through her conflicted conscience, we witness Meanwell's transformation from a powerless English waif to a mythic American who ultimately chooses wilderness over the civilization she has experienced.

Four-Way Stop - Sherry Olson
If *Thank You* were the only prayer, as Meister Eckhart has suggested, it would be enough, and Sherry Olson's poetry, in her second book, *Four-Way Stop*, would be one. Radical attention, deep love, and dedication to kindness illuminate these poems and the stories she tells us, which are drawn from her own life: with family, with friends, and wherever she travels, with strangers – who to Olson, never are strangers, but kin. Even at the difficult intersections, as in the title poem, *Four-Way Stop*, Olson experiences – and offers – hope, showing us how, *completely unsupervised*, people take turns, with *kindness waving each other on*. Olson writes, knowing that (to quote Czeslaw Milosz) *What surrounds us, here and now, is not guaranteed*. To this world, with her poems, Olson brings – and teaches – attention, generosity, compassion, and appreciative joy.
—Carol Henrikson

Entanglements - Tony Magistrale
A poet and a painter may employ different mediums to express the same snow-blown afternoon in January, but sometimes they find a way to capture the moment in such a way that their respective visions still manage to stir a reverberation, a connection. In part, that's what *Entanglements* seeks to do. Not so much for the poems and paintings to speak directly to one another, but for them to stir points of similarity.

Body of Work - Andrei Guruianu
Throughout thirteen stories, Body of Work chronicles the physical and emotional toll of characters consumed by the all-too-human need for a connection. Their world is achingly common — beauty and regret, obsession and self-doubt, the seductive charm of loneliness. Often fragmented, whimsical, always on the verge of melancholy, the collection is a sepia-toned portrait of nostalgia — each story like an artifact of our impermanence, an embrace of all that we have lost, of all that we might lose and love again someday.

Fomite
Burlington, Vermont

Dons of Time - Greg Guma
"Wherever you look...there you are." The next media breakthrough has just happened. They call it Remote Viewing and Tonio Wolfe is at the center of the storm. But the research underway at TELPORT's off-the-books lab is even more radical -- opening a window not only to remote places but completely different times. Now unsolved mysteries are colliding with cutting edge science and altered states of consciousness in a world of corporate gangsters, infamous crimes and top-secret experiments. Based on eyewitness accounts, suppressed documents and the lives of world-changers like Nikola Tesla, Annie Besant and Jack the Ripper, Dons of Time is a speculative adventure, a glimpse of an alternative future and a quantum leap to Gilded Age London at the tipping point of invention, revolution and murder.

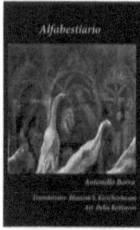 

Alfabestiario
AlphaBetaBestiario - Antonello Borra
Animals have always understood that mankind is not fully at home in the world. Bestiaries, hoping to teach, send out warnings. This one, of course, aims at doing the same.

The Consequence of Gesture - L.E. Smith
On a Monday evening in December of 1980, Mark David Chapman murdered John Lennon outside his apartment building in New York City. The Consequence of Gesture brings the reader along a three-day countdown to mayhem. This book inserts Chapman into the weekend plans of a group of friends sympathetic with his obsession to shatter a cultural icon and determined to perform their own iconoclastic gestures. John Lennon's life is not the only one that hangs in the balance. No one will emerge the same.

Sinfonia Bulgarica—Zdravka Evtimova
Sinfonia Bulgarica is a novel about four women in contemporary Bulgaria: a rich cold-blooded heiress, a masseuse dreaming of peace and quiet that never come, a powerful wife of the most influential man in the country, and a waitress struggling against all odds to win a victory over lies, poverty and humiliation. It is a realistic book of vice and yearning, of truthfulness and schemes, of love and desperation. The heroes are plain-spoken characters, whose action is limited by the contradictions of a society where lowness rules at many levels. The novel draws a picture of life in a country where many people believe that "Money is the most loyal friend of man". Yet the four women have an even more loyal friend: ruthlessness of life.

My Father's Keeper - Andrew Potok
The turmoil, terror and betrayal of their escape from Poland at the start of World War II lead us into this tale of hatred and forgiveness between father and son.

Fomite
Burlington, Vermont

Unfinished Stories of Girls—Catherine Zobal Dent
The sixteen stories in this debut collection set on the Eastern Shore of Maryland feature powerfully drawn characters with troubles and subjects such as communal guilt over a drunk-driving car accident that kills a young girl, the doomed marriage of a jewelry clerk and an undercover cop, the obsessions of a housecleaner jailed for forging her employers' signatures, the heart-breaking closeness of a family stuck in the snow. Each of Unfinished Stories of Girls' richly textured tales is embedded in the quiet and sometimes violent fields, towns, and riverbeds that are the backdrop for life in tidewater Maryland. Dent's deep love for her region shines through, but so does her melancholic thoughtfulness about its challenges and problems. The reader is invited inside the lives of characters trying to figure out the marshy world around them, when that world leaves much up to the imagination.

Writing a review on Amazon, Good Reads, Shelfari, Library Thing or other social media sites for readers will help the progress of independent publishing. To submit a review, go to the book page on any of the sites and follow the links for reviews. Books from independent presses rely on reader to reader communications.

www.ingramcontent.com/pod-product-compliance
Lightning Source LLC
Chambersburg PA
CBHW030331080526
44584CB00012B/804